# ABOUT FACE

*3 Badass Tips for an Awesome Military Transition*

**by Josh Coker**

# Copyright

About Face 2nd Edition

Copyright © 2018 by Story Ninjas

All rights reserved. This book or any portion thereof may not be reproduced or used in any manner whatsoever without the express written permission of the publisher, except for the use of brief quotations in a book review.

# Contents

| | |
|---|---|
| Copyright | 2 |
| Contents | 3 |
| INTRODUCTION | 5 |
| TIP ONE | 13 |
| TIP TWO | 21 |
| TIP THREE | 28 |
| BONUS ROUND! | 34 |
| Thank You From Story Ninjas | 40 |
| Other Books by Story Ninjas | 40 |
| About Story Ninjas | 40 |
| RESOURCES | 45 |

# INTRODUCTION

## Why this is important to you now.

*"I have a bad feeling about this..."*

*- Han Solo, Star Wars*

If you're anything like I was during my transition, you're probably scared to death about switching over to the civilian sector. Like countless veterans throughout the decades, you have no idea what to expect. How will you take care of your family? How will you pay your bills? Feed your kids? Do you have what it takes? Can you find another job? Where should you start? How do you add up to the competition? What if you don't have the skill sets they're looking for? What will you do if you can't find a job? And the list goes on, and on.

In short, your transition is the oncoming apocalypse.

If you don't get this right, you're doomed to a life of eating Ramen, wearing 2-week-old underwear, and selling your all worldly possessions (read: xbox and childhood comic books) just to survive.

At least that's what you've jedi-mind-tricked yourself into believing.

Well, let me start off by saying, "Dude (or dudette), just *chillax...*"

Like Dorothy setting out to find the Wizard of Oz, you're jumping at shadows. Concerned more about the proverbial lions, and tigers, and bears (Oh my!), than the actual yellow-brick-road that lies ahead.

These can be troubling times, yes. Especially with force reduction taking place across all services. If you're weren't planning on getting out (or your lazy ass procrastinated up until this moment...), you might be in a bit of a mad-scramble trying to work things out. But the good news is, things are never as bad we imagine. Not to mention, your whole military career has been preparing you for this exact situation. **Let's face it: no matter if you were an analyst, loadmaster, or pilot, you constantly moved from place to place; adapting to changes, working** under deadlines, and making difficult decisions.

**Your transition is no different.**

**Same. Same.**

Nevertheless, have no misconception, you're not in Kansas anymore. Whether you served for two months, two years, or two decades, the military indoctrinated (ahem, immersed…) you into a specific culture. One that thrives on honor, discipline, and sacrifice. They fed you, clothed you, and told you where (and sometimes when) to sleep. They took care of your medical, college, and housing costs. In a sense, the military was sort of your second set of parents. Some of you have spent more of your lives sheltered under the mother eagle's shadow (yes, that was a deliberate "merica" reference), than you have outside of the nest. But now it's finally time to spread your wings and fly.

The problem is, it's a great big world out there, and nothing in the civilian sector seems quite right..

As you embark on your journey, you're going to see job descriptions with words that appear to be written in a foreign language. None of the qualifications seem to match your experience bullet-for-bullet, so you start to hyperventilate as images of flipping burgers flash through your mind. Right about this time you get a tingling sensation in your head. Some call this a headache, others call it culture shock. But just remember, before basic training you survived nearly two decades in this world. It's just going to take a little time to re-adjust; like in *The Lion King*, when Simba comes back to the pride all grown up. He doesn't realize how much he's changed, and how powerful he's become. He has to readjust and figure out where he fits in this new paradigm.

And while I can't not say that things won't get a bit confusing (like a triple negative), **I can guarantee that you have all of the tools necessary to navigate the upcoming terrain.**

### GANGNAM STYLE? NOPE, MY STYLE.

As you've probably already surmised, I don't hold anything back. I like my writing like I like my gumbo; spicy and satisfying. So if I pepper in a few sharp words along the way, it's only to get the point across.

Does that mean I'm going to bombard you with f-bombs for

the next 20-ish pages?

No.

Well maybe, one or two...

But, it's for your own EFFING good!.

If you want to look at it another way, let's say you were about to drive your car off of a cliff. Which would you rather:

1) I calmly explain to you the theory of gravity and detail the risk factors. Then ask you politely to slow down and be careful.

OR

2) I scream your name at the top of my lungs and say, "STOP YOU SILLY BASTARD!!!" ***flails arms*** "YOU'RE GOING TO DIE!!!"

When lives are on the line, you don't sugar-coat sh*t.

And yes, in a sense, your life *is* on the line.

The decisions you're about to make, are going to affect you and your family for years to come. As your mentor, it's my job to care about you enough to tell you when you're effing-up. Hence the title *About Face*. As most of you know, this is the military marching command used to change a troop's direction if they're heading the wrong way. **The purpose of this book is to identify common pitfalls, and turn you toward the right course of action.** It's my duty. Nay, dare I say an obligation, to guide you away from the common mistakes most veterans make.

I'm also an old school storyteller and I like to use metaphors to get my point across. Kind of like Plato, except less beard and more blazer. As a tech-savvy 30-something that grew up in the 80's, I sprinkle lots of comic book/video game references throughout the narrative. Jesus did this too, when teaching his disciples. He spoke about shepherds of sheep and fishers of men. Similarly I use a modern-day tone, with iconic examples to connect you with larger concepts. The main point is, you either love my writing, or you hate it. If you've stuck with me this far, I'm going to assume you find my content congruent with your reading predilections (good choice, btw).

So buckle up. Sh*t's about to get real!

**WHO WILL BENEFIT FROM THIS BOOK?**

The easy answer is **YOU**.

But, if I was to answer this with my serious face on, then I would submit the following response:

This book was written primarily with military members in mind. Its goal is to help service members make a smooth transition into the civilian workforce. As I mentioned before, the reason I've titled it *About Face* is because this book identifies common pitfalls that military members make as they trek into the unknown jungles of the corporate sector. The tips herewithin will help you change direction before you run into monstrous problems.

**VETERANS/JOB SEEKERS:** However, that's not to say these tips couldn't be helpful to vets who've already changed careers, or anyone who plans on switching jobs in general.

**ACTIVE DUTY PERSONNEL:** For troops still serving, this material will give you a good idea of what to expect and allow you to implement strategies that will facilitate your future transition.

**SUPERVISORS:** Supervisors benefit as well. For the leaders out there, this is a good tool to assist your subordinates during this major life change. Say you have a troop who's contemplating separation. The book provides insight into what choices they have. This will allow you to give appropriate advice so they can make the most informed decision possible.

**MILITARY SPOUSES:** For family members, this gives you a good idea of what to expect and insight to what your spouse has to deal with.

**NONSENSICAL COMMONSENSICAL**

None of this is rocket science. And there's a good chance some of the information is stuff you already know. But that's okay, because reinforcement is the superglue of the mind--it makes stuff stick.

The way the book is organized, you can read straight through, or just pick the chapters that "speak" to you. Whatever you decide, this is a quick read (25-ish pages). My hope is that you'll find one or two "gems" that you can bring into the marketplace and create something of value for your prospective employers/clients/customers.

# TIP ONE

## Wax On, Wax Off. Don't Take The Basics For Granted.

*"Wax on, right hand. Wax off, left hand. Wax on, wax off. Breathe in through nose, out the mouth. Wax on, wax off. Don't forget to breathe, very important." -- Mr. Miyagi, Karate Kid*

**Common Pitfall**

Do you guys remember the original Karate Kid movie? You know that scene where Mr. Miyagi has Daniel-Son wax his cars? Daniel thinks the old man is wasting his time, but he begrudgingly does it. Then, Mr. Miyagi has him paint the fence. And again, the boy wonders when they're going to start practicing karate. But he spends hours painting the wood. Eventually, Daniel gets so frustrated, he blows-up at Miyagi in a classic Mel Gibson-esque meltdown. But in a mind-blowing change of events (at least to a 4 year old), Mr. Miyagi demonstrates that all of these basic movements (wax on, wax off) were actually building the foundation for his first lesson: How to block.

(Interesting side note: For the first few years of my life, I believed my grandfather was Mr. Miyagi. Like the karate master, he was bald, a handymen, AND used manual labor as a form of teaching. Solid logic, right? But I digress...)

The point is...

**Like Daniel-Son, military members have a tendency of taking things for granted.** And no, I'm not talking about tax-payer's dollars. I'm talking about all the tools at your disposal. For example: McDonalds, KFC, and Taco Bell may not be appealing right now, but spend six months overseas--where seaweed and insects are on the menu--and suddenly a Big Mac is a *BIG DEAL*. Same thing holds true for deodorant, toothbrushes, and clean underwear. But when it comes to their career, service members put-off the Transition Assistance Program (TAP) till the last minute.

Vets take it for granted because, like Daniel-Son, they think the basics are a waste of time.

Nothing could be further from the truth.

For those who are unfamiliar with the term, TAP Class - the U.S. Military's Transition Assistance Program - was created by the government to help service members crossover to the civilian sector. With roughly 300,000 vets separating each year, there's no doubt that a program was needed. It's a week long instructional course. The goal is to lay the foundation for your shift into the private sector. Certified instructors coach service members through the intricacies of resume preparation, interviews, professional attire, and other job-related topics. **татA TAP is one of the most useful separation resources the military provides service members.**

If the Three Little Pigs taught us anything, it's that you need a solid foundation.

Can you be a master chef if you don't know how to cook an egg?

No.

Same thing goes for jobs. Will a prospective employer see you as a top performer if you don't know how to write a resume, or give an interview?

No.

Nevertheless service members are notorious for putting this off until the last minute. I mean why not? Isn't writing a resume basically the same as drafting evaluation bullets? Aren't interviews a lot like going to a military board? Wearing a suit is the same as wearing blues, right? So why bother, *right*? If you already know the stuff, then you don't need the class to teach you. R~i~ght?

WRONG!

That's like saying a Jedi doesn't need a lightsaber, or a Time-Lord doesn't need sonic screw-driver. TAP Class is one of the greatest tools at your disposal.

**TAP Class provides a launchpad for your new job.** Even if you're not planning to leave the service any time soon, much of the information will help you grow your professional portfolio. The firmer your foundation, the easier your transition. Ultimately, this frees up more time for you to focus on the things that matter.

*Repetition is one of the oldest and most effective forms of teaching/learning.*  **Repetition is one of the oldest and most effective forms of teaching/learning.**

REPETITION IS ONE OF THE OLDEST AND MOST EFFECTIVE FORMS OF TEACHING/LEARNING.

So, in case the horse isn't dead enough already, I intend to beat it some more...

**Reversal**

Occasionally, timing and backlog won't allow you to sign up for a class. For example, I had a conversation with few sailors not too long ago, who told me the Baltimore-Washington region was booked six months out.

SIX MONTHS!

To give you some perspective, that's 182 days, or 4,368 hours, or 2,620,920 minutes.

OR... 15,724,800 seconds.

The point is, you have to prepare a looooong time in advance.

In the event you can't get a class before you separate, don't stress. Regardless of availability, you have a plethora of other resources, including this helpful holocron-ish guide--filled with Jedi Master wisdom--to guide you in the ways of the Force. Check out the references section at the end of this book for a sh*t-ton of informative links to aforementioned resources.

**About Face**

1. **Notify Your Sup:** Discuss transition with supervisor. DoD suggests 12 months in advance for separation and 24 months in advance for retirement.
2. **Notify Your Family:** Moreover, common sense dictates that you should keep your significant other (read: spouse/cohabitant/lover/mistress/mister and pet plant, "Leafy") apprised of any situation where you may have to move or become unemployed (pro-tip: this counts for any ex-wives/husbands--especially if you pay them child support). You'd be surprised how many people wait until the last minute to have these conversations. I could be wrong, but your significant other will probably find this information important. As in, if you don't tell them, you're in the doghouse *important*.

3. **Notify Operational and Administrative Commands:** Give them a heads-up that you plan to attend TAP Class. This has the added benefit of reminding management that they have to find a replacement for you. The sooner the better. That way you and the poor sap who's taking over your spot gets sufficient time for pass-down.

4. **Before TAP Class:** Sign up for Informed Decision Brief and Pre-separation Brief. This is a necessary evil (read: mandatory fun) and must be accomplished before signing up for TAP. This could add 2-4 weeks of wait time, so go sign up *now*.

5. **TAKE NOTES AND ASK QUESTIONS:** There's no point in reading this G-D book, or doing all this G-D preparation, or going to the G-D class, if you don't get the G-D information that you need for your G-D transition. So, take some G-D notes and ask some G-D questions.

## Conclusion

*We make sacred pact. I promise teach karate to you, you promise learn. I say, you do, no questions. --Mr. Miyagi, Karate Kid*

Just sign up for the damn class already... Worst case scenario, you'll get a week off of work.

For further information, refer to my YouTube video on the subject: https://www.youtube.com/watch?v=YpPmx-Pv-ak&index=6&list=PLpyZQMxyU6KkqblensdHoLMbo6gCofWYi

# TIP TWO

## Get thyself a Batmobile (and other cool tools).

*"Ooh. Whatcha sneaking with you, Bats? Oh come on, tell me, tell me. Batarangs? Batclaws? Ooh! Batsnacks?" --The Joker, Batman: Arkham Asylum*

**Common Pitfall**

STATEMENT: Batman, (AKA Bruce Wayne) is the most badass superhero in all comicdom. (<-- That's a period, indicating the end of the conversation)

More badass than Flash or Wonder Woman. And yes, even more badass than Superman (that's right, I said it).

Why?

Because unlike Supes, or Flash, or the rest of the Justice League, his badassery comes from within. He's just a regular guy like you and I. He has no superpowers. He can't fly, or shoot frick'n laser-beams from his eyes. Instead Batman relies on his intellect and badass bat-gadgets to get the job done. He uses an impressive bat-bag of bat-tricks (baterangs, batmobiles, batbelts, and bat-etc..) to protect Gotham from the machinations of criminals, like the Joker.

Batman has different tools for different situations. Each of them tailored to the specific needs of the problem.

The same holds true for your new career.

TAP Class is just one tool in the toolbox. Like the Batsuit, you'll use it in almost every encounter. But there will be times where you'll need different, more advanced tools to face the challenges that are certainly lurking in the alleyways of your future. Of course there are several books out there (like this one), and YouTube has a sh*t-ton of informative videos (like my YouTube Channel[1]) to help veterans with their transition.

The following are a few suggestions on how to increase your badassery:

1. **Read Books:** There are a ton out there. From interview

---
[1] https://www.youtube.com/user/Tipperdy/

tips, to social media management, and negotiating salary, there are a ton of books out there to help you out. I try to read one a month. This keeps me fresh and up-to-date with emerging strategies, technologies, and trends.

2. **Youtube:** If you're not much of a reader, then there's always videos. According to YouTube's statistics page, YouTube has over 6 billion hours of video. Believe it or not, 100 hours of video are uploaded to YouTube every minute! The great thing about Youtube and similar repositories is that they're updated daily with new information. The other added benefit is that you can search for very specific answers to very specific questions.

3. **VA Online Resources:** Although they're not always the most user-friendly, or up-to-date, sometimes you can find some real gems buried away in this material. Check out the "Resources" section at the end of this book for a few of these helpful links.

**REVERSAL**

Batman can't take every tool into battle. If he tried, he'd never leave the Batcave. Keeping Gotham safe is his priority. The same thing applies to you. Your mission is to get a job, not to cultivate so many skills that people start to call you Leonardo Da Vinci. Try to focus on the skillsets you need for the next few months. Have an interview coming up? Watch a few videos (or read a few books) that focus on most common interview questions. Then try to anticipate which topics might come up in conversation and write them down. Develope a few canned responses, and practice them over and over. Just like Batman practices his moves, you'll need to have your introduction; elevator speech; pitch; and several other key discussion points nailed down. Like a coffin. Hammer them hard, so you don't end up dead in the water.

Practice. Practice. Practice.

Practice so much you could say them in your sleep.

Practice with a friend, or a fox. Practice on a pillow or a box. Practice on a train, or on a plane. Practice everywhere Sam-I-Am. Practice while eating green eggs and ham.

Moreover, at some point Bats has to get down to business.

Even though you should cultivate multiple avenues, you should never lose sight of your primary objective: getting the job you deserve. This requires going out onto the mean streets and engaging people. You should always spend more time talking with prospective clients and employers than taking courses (more on this in the next chapter). All the preparation in the world isn't worth a G-D thing if you fail to put it into action. Identify what actions you can take to to develop your current skills and gain new ones. This will increase your overall value for prospective employers.

If you've already landed a job, don't stop there. You should be constantly expanding your arsenal, that way you're always ready for the next challenge.

**ABOUT FACE**

1. **Sidekicks and Allies:** Batman has friends. Alfred, Robin, Superman, etc... Talk to friends who had a successful transition. Speak with your supervisor/leadership and find out how to get started. Do not hesitate to use the people around you as resources.

2. **Research:** Get online and find out what steps you need to take both in your separation and to find a suitable job in the civilian sector.

3. **Resume:** When it comes to resumes, you need the "hot girl at a bar" reaction. You want employers lining-up to meet you. Don't assume you can achieve this on your own. Asking for help from a professional, will only help your odds. Whether it's a career coach, or how-to book, or online resources, make sure you research the best practices. And when your resume is complete, you can post it on the TAP website, which is currently located here[2].

4. **Take action:** Consider what things you could do this week to keep your focus on your career transition. Identify one or two sources that are already an easily accessible part of your daily life. Use these to learn more about relevant job search information. And, of course, watching the About Face series on my YouTube Channel [3] will always keep you informed on the latest transition tips, tricks, and tactics.

---

[2] http://www.taonline.com/FormsLogin.asp?/JobSeeker/ViewResumes.asp

[3] https://www.youtube.com/playlist?list=PLpyZQMxyU6KkqblensdHoLMbo6gCofWYi

# Conclusion

*Robin: "Where'd you get a live fish, Batman?"*

*Batman: "The true crimefighter always carries everything he needs in his utility belt, Robin." --Batman lecturing Robin*

The universe keeps expanding, the galaxies move, and solar systems shift, creating a ripple effect on all of space and time (down to the quantum level). The same is true for each and everyone one of us. Everything is constantly in motion. Every moment of every day, someone somewhere is innovating and stretching your industry's boundaries. The only way to stay relevant is to constantly grow; through training, practice, and preparation.

Never confine your activities to just one or two subjects. There are a multitude of options out there, and all you need to do is reach out and take advantage of them. By utilizing TAP, you're taking a great first step, but don't stop there. Success does *not* come from one massive leap, but from a series of small steps, taken one after the other.

# TIP THREE

## Avoid the "Bagginsez" Complex, My Precious.

*"Sorry! I don't want any adventures, thank you. Not Today. Good morning! But please come to tea – any time you like! Why not tomorrow? Good bye!"*

*--Bilbo Baggins, The Hobbit*

**Common Pitfall**

Most service members take on the "Bilbo Baggins" complex. They'd rather spend all their days moping at home, than going out on an adventure. Networking is about meeting real people, in real life, and making meaningful, mutually beneficial connections. Sure some of the characters you come across may seem like trolls. But others may end up surprising you. By forging alliances, you will not only significantly increase your chances of a successful transition, but you will also create opportunities where they otherwise wouldn't have existed.

**Remember, it's not a computer or a phone that's going to hire you, it's a person.** The ability to connect on a personal level is the number one skill when looking for a job. Employers don't hire a sheet of paper. They hire a person. Normally someone they consider trustworthy. Often this means getting a recommendation from a trusted friend/confidant. Therefore creating new relationships and cultivating existing ones is the key to long term success. Personal referrals are often what makes the difference between getting hired and being passed over. Unlike Bilbo, you don't have Elevnty-one years to figure this stuff out. You need to get to work and start slaying dragons now.

Sometimes it's as simple as going to an event with friends. Other times, it may require that you initiate a conversation with a stranger. And although that may seem intimidating, remember, they're just a person like you and I. Flesh and blood. No more, no less. I've got a few tips on universal greetings here.[4] Whatever it

---

[4] https://www.youtube.com/watch?v=Ps_64N4MfX4

takes to get yourself in front of other people, do it. Friends and family members will be happy to support you. If you've just moved or are visiting someplace new, go out and meet people. The internet is a great tool to find hot spots for all kinds of local activities.

**According to the U.S. Bureau of Labor Statistics, as many as 70% of jobs are the result of networking.** And according to recruiting blogs, that number may be as high as 85% when you consider jobs found through friends and family. That doesn't mean you won't find a job through the direct approach, it just means your odds are significantly improved when you network.

**There are plenty of ways to get out and make connections.**

**You can volunteer at events, engage with your local community, attend job fairs, and apply for internships.** Even if the connections you make don't lead to a job offer, you'll gain valuable experience that will help you down the road. Dealing with multitudes of people will cultivate your communication skills.

Over time you will accumulate countless reference points which will act act as building blocks for your job search. With these raw materials you will build a fortress of confidence, that will allow you to face any challenge.

**Would you rather sit around and stare at the walls all day? Or, would you rather go do something extraordinary?** Find a job that excites you and makes you feel like you're on an adventure, then go out and get it.

ABOUT FACE

**1. Step out of your comfort zone:** This can take many forms, but you literally have to take a step outside. You could talk to five new people everyday. Sign up for a convention. Join toastmasters, or a book club. Take an art class. Visit prospective employers and ask the employees questions about the company. Maybe you volunteer at a community event. The options are endless, but you have to get out of your house and into the world.

**2. Take someone with you:** Take a lesson from Gandalf. If you're going to head out into the world on an adventure, bring some friends. Try to surround yourself with people who will help you achieve your goal. If leaving your comfort zone is intimidating, take a friend with you. There has to be at least one person you can convince to join your cause.

**Conclusion**

> *"It's a dangerous business, Frodo, going out of your door," he used to say. "You step into the Road, and if you don't keep your feet, there is no telling where you might be swept off to."*
> *--Frodo Baggins about Bilbo, The Fellowship of the Ring, Three is Company*

Make it a point to breakout of your comfort zone every day. This will push you past your limits and allow you to expand your network as well as your confidence. If you never get out there, you're robbing yourself of countless opportunities, not to mention the adventure of life. Who knows what exciting challenges are waiting for you. Or what amazing people you'll meet on the other end. Most importantly, consider how much will you learn about yourself while going through this process.

# BONUS ROUND!

## Test Your Might!

*"Flawless Victory"*
*--Shang Tsung, Mortal Kombat*

The 90's were a decade filled with all kinds of cool stuff. *No Fear* T-shirts, snap bracelets, and AOL. Movies like Ninja Turtles II, The Sandlot, and The Mighty Ducks. AND don't forget jamming out to Ace of Base on the bus-ride back from school ***Holds invisible microphone to mouth and lip-syncs *I Saw The Sign****

Oh man, the memories...

One of the biggest sensations to sweep the nation was the introduction of arcade fighting games. Street Fighter 2, Tekken Tag, Marvel vs Capcom. It was a pre-pubescent teen's paradise!

And despite all of this testosterone filled amazingness, one game rose above all the others and claimed the throne: *Mortal*

*Kombat.*

Violent, controversial, and over-the-top are just three adjectives--albeit understatements--to describe the most iconic fighting game of all time.

In 1991, spine-ripping fatalities and spike-impaling pits took arcades by storm and teleported Mortal Kombat to the number one spot in the fighting game paradigm. Mortal Kombat decimated its competition (**k**ompetition?) and changed the industry forever. Part of this was due to the ungodly amounts of blood and gore, sure. But if Ed Boon and the creators at Midway relied solely on the headline-inducing violence, they would have quickly lost their foothold in the industry. The reason, they've been able to dominate the competition for nearly three decades, is because they've consistently given fans more than a fighting game. Whether it's badass characters (ice, fire, lightning wielders--and a dude with frick'n swords coming out of his arms), interactive environments (uppercuts into a spiked ceilings, pools of acid, and pits of impaling blades), or hundreds of unique moves (split punch-to-the-groin, scissor kicks to the face, bicycle kick "hiyimiyooowidwayaaaa!"), they've constantly pushed the envelope.

As a pre-teen who probably shouldn't have been playing the game, one of the things I remember the most (aside from Scorpion's char-broiling fatality), was the "test your might" bonus rounds. This mini-game gave gamers a break from fighting, by allowing their avatars to break boards, stones, and anvils. Later renditions included a human head, marble, iron, amber, pearl, sapphire, and diamond. Whichever player chops with the most power wins. Although it may not sound like much, it was tiny additions like these that yanked the fans back like a scorpion-spear (GET OVER HERE!), decade after decade.

Now, I can hear you asking me, "Josh, what are you suggesting? You want me to go out and uppercut the sh*t out of my clients?"

NO.

At least not literally.

(Pro-tip: Listen up my ninja, even though some a-holes out there deserve a good kick to the taco, jail is not a fun place to spend the weekend.)

Rather, what I'm saying is that you should always strive to give more than what's expected (like this extra chapter of amazingness). No matter what industry you're in, all companies, clients, and employers are looking for the best investment for their money.

Let me rephrase.

People buy stuff (or hire someone) when they feel as though they're getting MORE value from the commodity, than the money they spend on it. So if you only meet expectations, if you're only do what's within the duty description, then you'll quickly find yourself falling down the fiery chasm of doom where the spikes-of-rejection are waiting to impale the sh*t out of you. In order to have a "flawless victory" when it comes to your job transition, you're going to have "kill it". You MUST set yourself far apart from the competition.

This means more than just showing up early for an interview with your resume.

Just because you didn't show up late, and you know how to

write words on a sheet of paper, doesn't mean an employer's going to shower you with hundred dollar bills. (On a related note: While you're looking for a job, don't go to the strip club. DO NOT. This is a bad idea. Unless you plan to be a dancer, strip clubs are not conducive to your financial stability. Alcohol + strip club = bad life decisions). Now where was I... Oh yes, the interview. The five other candidates before you, just bored them with the same exact sh*t. Employers want to see what sets you apart.

They don't want vanilla.

They want the X factor.

They don't want Street Fighter, or Tekken, or Killer Instinct (bet you don't remember that last one do you.....).

They want Mortal-F*cking-Kombat.

This means following-up with emails and phone calls. It means that if they're hesitant to hire you, you volunteer to work at special events. Or, offer to intern--for free--before they bring you on board. Give them a sample of your product so they can see what you can do.

Go the extra mile.

Then leave them wanting more.

For some of you, this could mean writing a book/pamphlet/how-to guide on something you have expertise in (preferably a related field to your industry, not World of Warcraft). I guarantee that none of the competition is doing this. Design a website that has pictures (or videos) of you in action, either working within relevant skillsets, or interacting with other people. **Show them that you're far more than a automaton that performs robot tasks, but rather an expert in your field who has a personality and cares about their company. Be someone that takes their career seriously. You're not just there to fill space. You're there to create space.** You eat, sleep, breath, and crap in that space because it's your space. You own it.

Don't just meet the standard, set the standard.

If you can do that. Then the sky's the limit.

## Thank You From Story Ninjas

Story Ninjas Publishing would like to thank you for reading this story. We hope you found value in our book and would love to hear your feedback. Please provide your constructive criticism in a review on Amazon. Also feel free to share this book with your friends through the various social media platforms.

## Other Books by Story Ninjas

Story Ninjas Publishing hopes you enjoyed this book. Check out our Amazon page for more products you may be interested in.

## About Story Ninjas

Story Ninjas Publishing is an independent book publisher. Our stories range from science fiction to paranormal romance. Our goal is to create stories that are not only entertaining, but endearing. We believe engaging narrative can lead to personal growth. Through unforgettable characters and powerful plot we portray themes that are relevant for today's issues.

You can find more Story Ninja's products below.

*Follow Story Ninjas!!!*
Website: www.story-ninjas.com
Email: Story-Ninjas@Story-Ninjas.com
Twitter: @StoryNinjas
Youtube: @StoryNinjas

Amazon: Story Ninjas
G+: +Story Ninjas
Facebook: StoryNinjasHQ
LinkedIn: Story-Ninjas
Blogger: Story-NinjasHQ

# About The Author

Josh Coker is the author of the Modern Monomyth series and several works of fiction. He is a co-founder of Story-Ninjas Publishing and also the creator of online courses such as Reciprocal Narrative Infrastructure, Thematic Resonance, and Subconscious Storytelling.

Josh is known as a premiere writing mentor and consultant, exclusively serving high-fee clients in the commercial fiction industry. He is also known for creating successful story narratives that increase audience engagement while delivering impactful thematic lessons. For the last 15 years, Josh has been writing, publishing, and researching fiction. He has helped outline, write, edit, publish and also market hundreds of books.

You can learn more about Josh by checking out his youtube channel, or his blog. Feel free to follow Josh on social media, to find to get updates on all of his latest projects:

FOLLOW JOSH!!!

- Instagram: http: @Joshumusprime
- Twitter: https: @Joshumusprime
- Facebook: Josh Coker
- Snapchat: @Joshumusprime
- Amazon: Josh-Coker
- Youtube: Josh Coker
- Blog: The Polymath Man

# RESOURCES

- http://www.dol.gov/vets/gils/records/000216.htm
- http://www.dol.gov/vets/programs/tap/tap_fs.htm
- http://www.militaryonesource.mil/phases-retiring?content_id=267523
- http://www.benefits.va.gov/VOW/tap.asp
- http://www.dtic.mil/whs/directives/infomgt/forms/eforms/dd2648-1t.pdf
- http://www.military.com/veteran-jobs/career-advice/military-transition/transition-assistance-program-help.html
- http://www.dol.gov/vets/programs/tap/DOLEW-Participant-Guide%28Oct%202012%29.pdf
- http://www.afpc.af.mil/lifeandcareer/transition.asp

www.ingramcontent.com/pod-product-compliance
Lightning Source LLC
Chambersburg PA
CBHW072048190526
45165CB00019B/2218